Count It All
JAMES 1:2

Poetry by
MARY M. MUELLER

www.xulonpress.com

DEAR READER,

May you peruse lazily through this poetry and feel the joy-bubbles burst on your finger tips. Please, leave your expectation on the porch and walk barefoot through the puddles as my dog Belle does. You may even want to sniff the grass and drink the new rain water. I don't mind. I am still. I am blessed by being full of emptiness. You may sit with me if you like.

Consider that God and I converse somewhat randomly. If there is a place where you might wonder who said what to whom, just add: *and God said...*somewhere. You'll untangle the word-knot. Please, leave it with a bow on top. Thanks.

~ Mary Mueller
May 2014

ACKNOWLEDGEMENTS:

A huge thank you to Betty Scott for her editing skills and gentle encouragement. I would be remiss not to mention Deb Ivancovich and my gratitude to her for inspiring me and reminding me to always, always point to Jesus. Bless you, my dear friends Elaine, Faye and Reba for being in my corner when my corner was a mere shadow at noonday. May God open His Joy-gates upon each of you. And thank you to Xulon Press for your assistance in publishing. Most important of all is the gratitude I feel toward our Creator Who blesses me with His Words and allows me the privilege of praise.

DEDICATION

To all those who are confused by God's gift of joy.
There's no explaining it; it is just there in all
the unexpected places.

TABLE OF CONTENTS

The ability to find joy in the
world of sorrow and hope at
the edge of despair is woman's
witness to courage and her
gift of new life to all.
~Miriam Theresa Winter
North American Medical
Mission Sister

Part I

ME…JOY

True joy, we must know, is a resident
of the heart. It is a gift from God
that is a part of belief and a partner
to peace. I so welcome joy to take
the place where sadness once lived
and I give joy permission to teach me
to play again.

A Crumbling

The facade is crumbling
    brick by brick, board by board
No reason to hide
    and a BIG reason not to
Much as I would
    like to think
False cover-up
    is gone
It lingers yet
    won't let me forget
Threads of this world
    still intertwine
        with mine

Hello! I ride
    a trike
My hair is slowly turning
    white-not pink or purple
As is the fad
    but not my own
Any more than texting or
    getting answers
        from an iPhone

I actually still read BOOKS!
   not Sony readers,
      Kindles or Nooks
And write whimsical poetry...
   say...look there

The wind-eraser missed
   a bit of cloud dust
A long dark charcoal line
   slashes the sky-board
Streaks and sweeps
   show up the messiness
      of the wind-eraser
Stuff like that
   fills my days
As I pick joy
   from the joy-tree
That sprang up over night
   on my rooftop

Stranger

He stood right in my path
        legs apart, hair wild
His voice was loud
        and he was gesturing
I rode right up to him
You're right in her way
        someone called

As if I couldn't ride around
        Well, it's not every day
An oldish woman
        on a trike rides up
And says: *May I give you a copy*
        of my book?
He took the proffered gift
        What else could he do?

Apparently used to hand outs
        he said what
He thought was expected:
        God bless you
How come he got it? came the call
        followed by a snide
                'cause he's black?

Only as far as the fountain
U-turn
Hand extended to the scruffy
snide-speaker
And how come I get one?
'cause I'm white? Right!
There he was
dirty, front tooth missing

Worlds for a moment mingled
in our laughter
What he didn't know
a Christian tract
slept in the back
Along with a ten dollar bill
It's not much
but maybe...

Maybe he will read
the book and
Find the tract and the words
I could not say
Maybe a small seed will sprout
in his dry ground
Maybe the Holy Spirit will smile
and tip His watering can

Carelessness

Thank You, Lord
   for guardian angels
One stopped the car
   that I swerved
      in front of
The brakes squealed
   no one knew of the angel
But I did

Help me, Lord, to beware
   of euphoric joy
      that makes me careless
Can't I have both
   wild joy AND safety?
      OK. I'll work on it

But to contain joy...
   I don't know
It wants to seep under doors
   like water
Fill rooms
   as sunshine

Surround
   as the very air
    we breathe
I just don't know about
   containing joy

Perhaps I should work
   on safety instead

Yesterday evening I wrote a poem entitled *Stranger*. In bed I completed reading Macrina Weiderkehr's *Seasons of Your Heart*. One of her last poems was *Jesus...Stranger*. It stopped me dead in my mental meanderings. This verse came to mind along with a new thought:

> *Whatsoever ye do unto the least*
> *of these, my brethren, ye have*
> *done it unto Me.*
> ~Matthew 25:40 (KJV)

Was this unnamed stranger one of the least of these? Was he Jesus in skin? Although I had some incomplete view of evangelism, perhaps Jesus was working on my heart as well. Do we see our fellow man as bearers of the image of God...whoever it is...the pastor, the lady beside me on the park bench, the homeless black man with the wild hair? Somewhere in their soul/spirit is that image. It may be sleeping or dormant just now waiting to be awakened.

By me? By all of us. Oh, I am so humbled by this awesome privilege. Evangelism.

German refugees during WWII.
Are things so different now?

He who sows, even with tears, the
precious seed of faith, hope, and love,
shall doubtless come again with joy,
bringing his sheaves with him,
because it is the very nature of that
seed to yield a joyful harvest.
　　　~Richard Cecil
When you see your brother, you see
the Lord, your God.
　　　~ Apollo (500 AD)
　　　　Desert Father

21

AM/PM

PM What do I know
   of homeless?
Bearded faces
   haunted eyes
How can I feed you
hope-words
When you haven't eaten
   properly in days?

I feel pathetically
   inadequate
To evangelism's
   task
My world: protected
   more than enough
What do I know
   of any of this?

AM

I know the wonderful
   Love of Jesus
I know His promises
    to bear every sin
    to go before, with, after
    to supply every need
    to do what we cannot
    to feed hope
    to fill empty eyes
    to paint joy in broken hearts
All I really need to know
   is Jesus!!!

Jesus doesn't promise us worldly success
   He promises Himself
Jesus doesn't promise riches
   He promises a rich life in Him
Jesus doesn't promise us easy lives
   He promises to be with us

~Jefferson Bethke from *Jesus Religion*

A Cluttered Life

My life is so cluttered
   with worry
What others may think
   of me
Reliving past mistakes
   anticipating more

There's only a sliver of space
   reserved for Joy
Sometimes even this gets filled
   with superficial happiness
Joy lies forgotten
   a broken toy upon the shelf
     ...of self

Joy! Arise!
   set the song free
To fill the skies
   the release of it
Bursting within me

Clean up my cluttered life
loose entangling weights
I, too, rise
with the song
Sprinkling Jesus-joy
as I go

Jesus-Eyes

Do you have Jesus-Eyes
   that see into the soul?
Can you feel that
   same compassion
      Jesus felt?
Do you desire to give
   a healing touch
      to a leper?
I want to have
   Jesus-Eyes
To envision potential
   from awkward beginnings
To Love unconditionally
   when hurt bars the door
      and self begs recognition
To forgive
   the clumsiness of others
Who blurt with no thought
   who don't know
      the rocks in my shoes
To be kind within
   the storm of words when
      kind looks like tough
Do you want to have
   Jesus-Eyes?
The prerequisite...
   a Jesus-Heart

The park was filled with people. One man with his beard and laden cart was by the walk where I rode. I stopped and asked if I could give him a copy of my book. For a moment I looked into the emptiness of his soul. I laid my book on top of his piled stuff. He said, "God bless you" in well-rehearsed beggar style. He was surprisingly young.

Lord, this is so hard. This man with his hope-less eyes needs so much more than I can give him.

Did you give him Me? That's OK. That's OK. Indirectly you did and you're still learning.

Learning to evangelize the homeless? But... but...that's so un-me. Help me, Lord, to be humble and to walk in shoes that aren't mine, ones that give me blisters: old tennis shoes, scuffed boots, no shoes...Teach me, Lord, to take off my shoes for this Holy Ground and be able to bear looking into hopeless eyes.

Morning Devotions

I love reading Oswald Chambers
　　　in the morning
Sometimes...three times
　　　just to get it!
Condense for the daily
　Songline
　　　a thought to live
　　　　that day by

OC is NOT easy
　　　to condense
Tuesday: Instill in me
　　　spiritual patience and pluck!
Patience is pretty good
　　　lots of practice
But spiritual
　　　pluck?

Like a guitar?
　　　like a chicken?
Like the black man with wild hair
　　May I give you a copy...?
Maybe...spiritual pluck takes on
　　　garments of humility
And leaves shoes behind

Wednesday: Seek first the Kingdom...
   but be carefully careless
      about everything else
What's this?
   I am NOT to take back
What I have given
   to God
Oh, it's hard to do
   Can't I keep a little pride

Or self-
   indulgence
Or harbor
   just a wee bit of disdain
Even in my thoughts
   I won't let on
OK...OK...

So this is what
   dying to self is all about
Not concealing one thing
   but let it all out
For this day, carefully careless,
   and the next
And the next...and the next

Joy-Bubbles

Has anyone ever caught
    a tumbleweed
That is in the pathway
    of the wind?
An insurmountable task
    I'd say

Or has someone held
    up his hand
To stop a snow slide
    to find he's been sucked
        in and under?
Just so, life slurps us up
    as a yummy milkshake

Right down to the chocolate
    dregs
As the woman with the jars
    of oil (II Kings 4:2-7)
My milkshake miracle
    doesn't seem to run dry

This sweet beverage
    of life
Continues to give off
    joy-bubbles
That effervesce
    upwards

Perhaps Jesus chuckles
    as He bursts
Rainbow-colored
    bubbles
Floating up
    and up...splash...
        and up

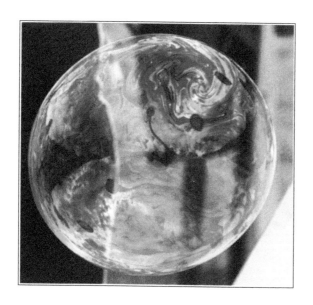

Did I Miss the Joy-bus?

Did I write about
   Joy-bubbles yesterday?
And miracle-milkshakes?
Isn't life interesting...
   I can't catch it
     by the tail
Wouldn't want to
   but still...

Here I am
   wondering if somehow
I missed
   the joy-bus
     for today
There just is no nice way
   to talk
     about pain
Incessant (it seems)
   grey-like rain

It's been sneaking
   up on me
     this Joy-stealer

Caught me napping
   too full
      to remember
To be carelessly
   careful
      with pain
Soooooo

Hello back pain
   did you know
      that I play bells
And ride a trike
   quite
      recklessly
Oh, you know...
   and came to
      remind me
But I have
   a secret
      that I will share

Joy does not
   reside in laughter alone
      or take a back seat
To back pain

Sometimes
    Joy curls up
        inside the heart
And waits in stillness
    for the traffic to pass
        or the light to change

This is where I am
    today
Not stuck in traffic
    just waiting
        for the Light

Lean into it

Lean into what?
   Pain
Cradle it a bit
   surround it with love
And warmth
   pain's not alone

After all you're there
   a part of you
You're not
   a part of pain
Hope hovers
   around the edges

Hope with
   Jesus-eyes
That crinkle in the corners
   even when
     laughter
Naps with the kitty
   in the basket

Drop of God

God sprinkled the earth
  one day
With birth-drops
  of creativity
One splashed upon
  my heart

I can barely contain
  the joy of it
And joy is just
  a tiny human word
For this mighty
  God-expression

Ideas flow (ha!)
  gush with flooding force
No dam can hold
  them back
No book can hold
  their content

A new phrase
  coins itself
"Go with the
  GOD-FLOW"

Who knows where it
    will take you

Just don't get
    left behind
Or allow head-hunters
    to scare you away
Persecution comes in forms
    we don't expect

Heed this
    clarion call
Hold fast!
    Stand tall!
The requirement...
    your ALL

Washed in a
    drop of God

God made a million, million doors
In the world for His love to walk
through. One of these doors is you...
One of these doors is you.
    ~Jason Gray

Yard Sale Aftermath

Such an idea
    reach out to your neighbors
With the age old question
    and who is my neighbor?
Well, many of my family
    offered a hand or two
And many of my neighbors
    (for I have MANY neighbors)
        followed through

Donation only
    the gift between you and God
Don't ask me
    I'm only a Love-conduit
You're on your own
    to go through it
        and do it

Donation recipient
    Agape House-homeless
We rally forth
    with a third party gift
The time is coming (I John 4:3)
    and indeed is already here

Hmmm
   a familiar ring
Is there perhaps
   a relationship
Between the Kingdom of God
   and my yard sale?

I wonder...
   take this leap with me
Is there perhaps
   a relationship
Between the Kingdom of God
   and life?

People-Puzzle Fit

This have and have-not
  of community
Opens our eyes
  to one another
Your haves
  and my have-nots
Seem to go
  together well

You have a wood saw
  my needs are small
Just two-three inches
  off the edge of a ledge
No sanding necessary
  no one will see
So nice of you to offer
  oh yes, I guess I asked

I have a sewing machine
    been a seamstress for years
I don't mind doing your mending
    or perhaps dry your tears
Oh, that's right
    some men don't cry
That must have been tears
    from the wears, my mistake

Just basic economics
    some might say:
My car/you're a mechanic
Your techy trend/my computer won't
    send
Behold my garden/what! you're a chef?

In so many ways we need each other
The bass harmonizes with the treble clef
God really had a
    Master design
That perfectly fits
    your piece
      with mine

Thread for Canvas

Hello? Hello?
       warehouse echoes
Rough wood tables
       harbor rugged
       heavy duty sewing machines
I looked askance at the table
       as I spread out my heavy
       lady-like CLEAN quilt

No? You don't sew
       this type of thing
You sew canvas for boats
Your machines
       chew it up, spit it out

Well, my dilemma remains
       too thick for me
       you don't want to...
Perhaps I could
       use one of your machines
So sorry, I didn't
       mean to scare you

Seventeen years you say
    your own business
Two children
    your eleven-year-old boy
        already an entrepreneur
You only have heavy duty
    thread for canvas

Oh! thank you
    so much!
Yes, around twice
    the second about ½ inch in
Here let me
    collect the pins

You think
I should use staples
Well, my pins are pretty worthless
    after you sew over them
No? I can't pay you?
    Are you sure?

Well, may I give you
        a copy of my book?
                my Jesus-book
Little do you know
        you are being handed
                an explosive from God
My quilt will last a long time
        a really long time
                thanks to your somewhat
        begrudged efforts

Your life may last forever...

God hath given to man a short
time here upon earth, and yet
upon this short time eternity
depends.

> ~Jeremy Taylor
> (1613-1667)
> Anglican Bishop and
> spiritual writer

All flesh is grass, and all its
loveliness is like the flower
of the field. ...When the breath
of the Lord blows upon it; surely
the people are as grass. The
grass withers and the flower
fades, but the Word of our God
stands forever.

> ~Isaiah 40:6-8 (NASB)

Mortality

Mortality stares at me
   with aching eyes
Back muscles
   spasm between aches
Behind my eyes
   lies the receding cave
    of weariness

     Throb
    Throb
    Throb

Stop at the Post Office
   between the doctor
    and X-ray
Most outgoing
   caring about one another
Why I like this community...
    Is this the self I know?
Better get to know
   this new me

   Throb-*j*
    Throb-*o*
      Throb-*y*

This can't be
   it's just not me
There's no joy
   peek-a-booing
from an ache
Ah, remember why you love...
   not yours but
for My sake

Love surrounds pain
   embraces joy
Exhilarates
   rejoices
     frolics with delight
Love blesses
   all...every day...
     every night

All things are possible
for those who love God...
     Romans 8:28

deligh t
   ex h ilerate
     r ejoice
  fr o lic
    b less

Every Bump

Hmmm, my back felt every bump
  on the way to the clinic
Well, now I know
  where the bumps are
Protime blood count low
  due to fresh garden veggies
Well, now I know the good things
  veggies do for body-works

Support hose
  hot, hot, hot
But my legs don't ache
  or breathe or tan or...
Hard to sleep
  at night
But when I do
  it's deep and dreamless

I can always look at stuff
  complain, detain,
    remain with
Increasing lines around
  a looking-down mouth

Or seek for something good
   it's got to be there...
     somewhere...
That gives laughter-lines
   and joy-wrinkles
     and a soaring spirit

I could quote James 1:2 quite
   out of context: *Count it all joy*
     and not understand at all
But in reality find it
   doesn't look like any joy
     I've ever seen before
This Jesus-Joy found in surrender
   perseverance under trial
     Jesus-strength in weakness
And seek to grasp
   what I cannot hold
     but believe with all my heart

This Jesus-Joy!

What life's About

What? Not more!
   a back brace?
It's that or
   bed rest for a week
Lord, I'm looking for You
    are you playing Job with me?

Oh, there's no game
    just what life's all about
I know nothing
   of Job's heartache
Of his anguish
   or his tears

My own loss
   diminished with the years
The hollow space I held
   so long
Has become the measure
   wherein births a song

Of spring, and life
   of Love and joy
The notes tremble
   with its newness
So I shall lift my eyes
   from back-braced woe

And trace instead the racing rainbows
   prism caught
     when sun peeks out
Beauty extends its hand to laughter
   joy splashes upon the wall
And I forget the woe of me
   in the wonder of it all

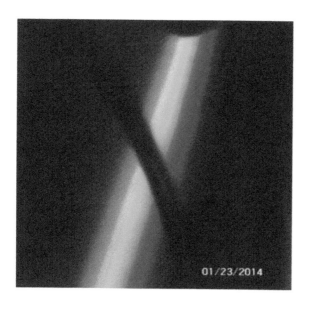

01/23/2014

Just Long Enough

This feeling
   flitted through
      my being
Leaving an upward turn
   in the corners
      of my mouth
And that joy-crinkle
   at the far edges
      of my eyes
Oh, linger
   I silently
      plead
But away
   and away
      not able to stay
Just long enough
   to have sprinkled
      Jesus-Joy dust
On my heart

There are times when the ecstasy of joy simply must expand to those around. I would be remiss not to share the glories God imparts. In every aspect of creation, if time is taken to inspect, there lies some semblance of God, waiting to be spied out. God rests quietly within our own hearts...waiting...waiting...

Enough

Peace presides
    How can this be?
His Presence
    ~only This~
And yet This only
    will always be
      enough

Happiness is the natural life of
man. Sheer Joy is God's and this
demands companionship.
~Thomas Aquinas
(1225-1274)
Italian Dominican Theologian

The neighbor cat, who still tippy-
toes quite well, gave me a look that
said: I was here first. Ha! We
tolerate each other. *Just stay out
of the flower beds; those seeds
don't need replanting and the soil
is just fine without your addition.*
He just continues to give that cat-
stare and lays down on the
sun-toasted bricks. MY bricks.
Ok, I'll share!

Part II

NATURE...JOY

May be...

The beginning
    of May
Did you know that horse chestnuts
    bloom white AND pink
It is worth putting up with
    all the prickly husks
Just to share the glory
    of their blooming

The lilacs are painting
    the landscape
Everywhere with white and lavender
    and bursting purple
Yesterday I heard a bird
    I didn't know
Calling *come nest,*
    come nest, come nest
I didn't answer
    one day I will

The Secret

My curly willow is sending
   me a sign language
Secret
   she's fast
I miss part
   I am happy...
To stretch...and
   be clothed...in green

Across the gulf of flowers
   and reaching beans
The funny mushroom-shaped
   alder dances and
     returns a greeting
Something in me says
   I must learn
The willow and the alder sign

Comes a whisper:
   You already know
Would the songs and the sign
   be there
If you weren't ready
   to interpret?
The tulips nod

I walked in my garden this morning at 5:45AM-slug hunting. Wouldn't you know, there were tent caterpillars in my curly willow. So there I was in my pink pajamas and lavender robe up on my raised bed cutting caterpillar nests out. I wonder if that will hinder the willow's signing. Well, better to be a little limbless than totally leafless, I think anyway.

And the caterpillars...? Well, there is this category in which slugs are mainly numbered. Tent caterpillars are in there too. I'm sure there are others that I don't know of and that's OK...like aphids and...

The Blooming Bush

Beside me there must be a whole hive
of bees in the lavender
blooming bush
I join them in their choice
of favorites
However, our expression
of appreciation differs

Warmer-sun peeks
in and out
When he hides
the breeze chills
My fountain sings and sings
its water song

And gently puts
me to sleep
Who naps at eleven-thirty
in the morning?
Since I was up at four
and heard the first birdie
and greeted pink sun-clouds

I guess I do!

Hello Morning

Hello morning
   still dusky in your
      beginning
The first birdie
   beats you with
      its brightness
But you follow
   not long
      after

A faint pink smear
   of lipstick
      left by a kiss
A momentary burst
   "poof"
      and gone
To leave a glowing
   that pierces
      my heart

If I could give
   a day
      to you

I'd give to you a day
   just like
      today
If I could sing a song
   for you, I'd sing a song
      to make you feel this way*

Words from a long-ago song

If I could share
   with you
      my heart
Fill you up
   with truth and joy
      that leaves no part
For pain
   or anguish
      tears or wrath

I'd sprinkle
   Jesus-Joy
      along your path!

*John Denver: Sunshine on my Shoulders

8:20 PM

I see tomorrow
   in the western clouds
There is a song
   in one
With hovering dark
   behind

Oh clouds, bring the rain
   but don't forget
      the song
And rain
   beloved of peas
      and beans
And all the lushness
   of spring

Don't forget
   the wind
      that breathes the song
And fills my heart
   with a thousand
Shades of
   Joy

As sunset comes
   the song-cloud pinkens
The dark take on
   a lavender lace edge
Tomorrow will be lovely
   whichever way
      the wind blows

Abigail and Belle

My cat Abigail
   sashays in
      as she always does
She makes a purring
   pass by me
      then turns to Belle
My Border Colley mix
   who is dreaming
      of rabbit trails
Belle never minds
   when Abigail
      kneads companionship

Both are black and white
   Abby's poof of softness
      snuggled up to Belle's summer cut
Always gives me pause
   there is a lesson here
      were we so caring...
We who are made
   in the image of God
      have distorted His Love
Into something
   unrecognizable...
      until redeemed!

I am redeemed, You set me free
So I'll shake off these heavy chains
Wipe away every stain, yeah
Now I'm not who I used to be
Oh God I'm not who I used to be
Jesus, I'm not who I used to be
'Cause I am redeemed
Thank God, redeemed
 ~Big Daddy Weave lyrics

Sunset Glory

Do you suppose
   there was a stumble
And sunset pink got spilled
   all over the sky
     and splashed into the sea?
Oh, the glory of it
   lingered until almost ten
Finally slipping away
   into the shadows of night
But a haunting beauty
   remains for the beholder

You'd think beauty wouldn't
   hurt so much

Breathless Joy

The stormy surface
   of the sea
Is on the bottom
   of the clouds
      Go figure!
Maybe it's the wind's
   fitful restlessness
That makes them
   so much the same

Yet all the trees are dancing
   in frenzied disunity
Shall we call it free-form
   or no-form or inform
Sorry, interpretation seems to have
   been blown away
      by that same wind
Only to return another day
   to let us know
      what the trees say

O wind, O wind
   between each gust
Your song of wild Joy
   whispers trust
To my soul

Imagine
   riding an updraft
Wings spread wide
   as an eagle's
Just a speck
   upon the lens of life
Breathless Joy, O Joy unspeakable
   released to reign
     in each believer's heart

Life is Beautiful

Night after night
   it just doesn't get any better (oh!)
Warm evening
   full moon later
Brilliant, brilliant
   sky in the west

But God reserves His very best
   that will never end
      never end
These evenings but a taste
   of what's to be
And all around
   we glimpse eternity

Life is beautiful
   so beautiful
      for now...for here
This present we hold
   so very dear
In actuality is but
   a broken mirror

That pales in His Glory!
   that pales in His Glory!

Slice of Day

Early morning blessings
    always greet me
Cool, cloud-filled skies
    await the sun to dissipate
Or the ever present wind
    to scutter them off to Canada

Already warm
    too hot promise for the afternoon
Good day
    to share
Would you care
    for a slice of today?

The crust is flaky gold
    with splashes of brilliance
You ask
    what kind of day?
Oh, each day is joy-filled
    with a generous sprinkle
        of laughter

Secret ingredients
    are only secret if kept
No secrets here!

Free...sunshine
   a coupon for dance lessons
      insurance for damage control

A special flavor
   you can't find anywhere else
The sweetness of Jesus
   tempered with tartness
      of honesty
And the salt
   of faithfulness

Such a Day!

A Place of Paradise

Hear the birdies praising
   Creator-God?
Swallows and cedar wax wings
   vie for first place
      in aerial acrobatics
The prize?
   a juicy insect...yum
The audience?
   those who watch in silence
      and wait...

God is enthroned in the praise
   of His people (Psalm 22:3)
The still beauty of this place
   alive with nature
Praises God
   as words cannot
Yet it is but a promise
   of the outrageously wonder-filled
Glory to come!

J ust another wonder that Jesus
   promises for those who believe in Him
     O ther-Love The commandment of Jesus
       to love God and love one another
         Y ou're rich in Love
          and Your heart is merciful

And we who lose ourselves in Your great Love
find eternal joy and peace. How amazing all
this is and beyond understanding!

Delight with Wonder

Delight slips down
   the apple blossom path
     with wonder
Their destination
   the pond
     where the goose family gathers
Today's
   the day

Wonder watches silently
   delight dances in expectation
Goslings plop into the pond
   nine, no, ten
     and yet one more
Follow-the-leader mom
   proud papa guards the tail

God's creation
   this year-by-year perfection
Nest lies hidden
   from predator-prying eyes
Each spring
   offspring reproduce
     the stately gander and his goose

Oh, wonder
of wonders
New life, new smells
new sounds
Delight not diminished
arises, expands
abounds!

Rose Garden

Belle and I sat
   in the Cornwall Rose Garden
The fragrance of roses
   wafts in a gentle breeze
      not heady but clean, sweet
The rose Cherry Parfait
   pie-cherry sauce poured
      over vanilla ice-cream
Rivals the yellow and peach beauty
   of About Face

The question arises:
Why does such beauty
   possess the repelling pokies
      (as my grandsons call them)
Well, here is the rose
   beautiful to behold
      sweet to smell
And yummy in your salad
   whatever that may be

If I saw a deer
   coming to bite my nose
     I'd want a thorn or two
Or if a cute bunny hopped by
   with a desire
     to nibble on my toes
I'd appreciate a thorn
   to protect my tender parts
And when it comes to a finger-stab
   or a sweater-snag
     I must remember

God's protections
   are different but available
     for us all
As I don the armor of God
   (Ephesians 6:14-17)
I know that He will protect
   my heart so I may not fall
On thorns
   or be gobbled up in greed
     or overwhelmed in need

Balm

Well, look at this
   not a breath of wind
The alder and the willow
   are still
      no secrets to share
They are saving these
   for another day
And I can wait
   this breathless evening cool
      entices me to linger

Sun sends long streaks
   through the spaces
      of the fence boards
Tall shadows
   disguise
      reality
The cool more eloquent
   than the sizzle
      of noonday
Speaks of refreshment
   passing appeasement
      of balm

So is our God
   our place of refreshment
     of cool balm
After the heat
   of battle
     whatever battle it may be
In time-perhaps-and space
   only the balm and cool remain
     battles won

From this viewpoint
   Peace the resident artist
     paints laughter
And–yes-joy splatters
   on this canvas
     of life

Blooming Scarlet

Sunflowers
   a golden choir
Beneath the curly
   willow tree
     that harbors
Bean vines with leaves
    as big as the outstretched
     fingers of my hand
Scarlet blossoms
   peer from their
     hiding height
Amid the curly willow's
   sheltering arms
A deceptive sight
   that curly willow
     blooming scarlet

Sharing

Eight chipping sparrows
   Spizella passerina
Eat birdseed
   on my deck rail
I sit in my bay window
   not a yard away

New babes with quivering wings
   even beg birdseed
One for you
   and two
      away Dad flew
Good parent
   that he is

Here's breakfast
   help yourself
It's free
   On me

If we so easily
　　share God's bounty
　　　with the birds
Can we not find
　　within ourselves
　　　upon our shelves
That to feed
　　another in need?

Transcient

Ginko leaves adorn
  the sky
No doubt wind-teased
  into perfection
    awaiting my inspection
Clouds so fickle
  in their shape
The sweep of sky-broom wind
  cloud streaks in its wake
Happy puffy cotton balls
  motionless it seems
    sheltering invisible angels
Driven streams
  toward Canada
    change with each blast
Oh, I love the clouds
  transient
    finger print of God

Hiding

This weeping day
    attempts to hide
The glistening joy
    of yesterday
But in each tear
    that falls
Is the remembrance
    of a laughing child

Although the grey
    breeds gloom
My heart denies it
    defies it
For the birth
    of tomorrow
Lies in the death
    of today

So I put my arms
    around this time
And hold it close
    call it dear
And know beyond
    a doubt
All is well
    for You are here

Pumpkins

Beneath the reaching golden sunflowers
    eight pumpkin seeds (Cucurbita pepo)
      flourish in the raised beds
Long vines escape
    over the edge
      and into the lawn
Baby pumpkins
    tiny hardballs nestle in the clover
      where the grass grows tall

Long yellow-orange blossoms
    invite each passing honeybee
      to taste and see
And on their seeking journey
    visit the little green ball
      at the end of the vine
To ensure
    a pumpkin there
      at harvest time

I can't quite taste the pumpkin pie
   looking at these
     small green globes
But some commercial growers can
   producing 1.5 billion
     pounds each year
Or plant for size
   with records of 1700 pounds
     Cinderella's coach for sure!

And some supply festivals
   with pumpkin chunkers
     who can throw the farthest
Oh, this popular North American native
   roots from Mexico
     thousands of years ago
Forever a favorite
   in our gardens
     on our tables

Thank You,
   Thank You, Lord
     for pumpkins!

Summer Sentinels

Lifting happy golden faces
   to the sun
Erect sentinels
   a welcoming portal
For every passing
   pollen-seeking bee
These emerge
   encased in golden dust
      for their treasure trove

Come fall
  heads get heavy
   with a load
Of shelled nutrients
  each one capable
   of renewing life
Unless marauding squirrels
  find it first
   in their busy cold-cashing
Or a passing flock
  migrating south
   stop for a seed-snack

Oh, the potential
  in a fertile seed
   to strengthen and repeat
That life
  so beautiful
   so sweet
God certainly knew
  what He was about
   and what was the need
When He placed
  a sunflower
   in a tiny seed

Artichoke Blooms

Blooming artichokes
   beautiful purple
      centers
Start peeking out
   with August
Mid August
   the outer sepals
      are full extended

Purple centers
   quite the bee attraction
      bottoms up
All the way to the base
   of the purple petals
Bees
   busy
      sharing
Five to a bloom
   better bee
      worth the while

Last year
   nineteen artichokes
Come August
   quite a
     color-splash
Some were stolen
   by the winter's
    cold
This year
   six remain still unique
    and lovely

Artichoke blooms

Jungle Garden

My jungle garden
   grows weeds
      as well as roses
A black cap chickadee
   hangs upside down
      on a bowed sunflower head
Pumpkins ripen
   beneath a fat
      sunflower
With pollen covered
   flower leaves
      dislodged by those worker bees
Scarlet runner beans
   are beaning
      from the curly willow branches
Zucchinis
   almost as big as baseball bats
      seem to balloon overnight
I wonder if kale
   and lettuce as big as dinner plates
      are still good to eat

I do love
   this jungle garden
      so do the crows!

Oh, and there are sweet peas
   still casting fragrance
      on all who pass
And...
   and...
      and...

Paint Brush Sweep

Bright clouds
    smile in the
        sunset sky
Just leave that wee space
    near the western edge
        for the golden sphere
To reach out with his
    pink-toned brush
        and sweep the heavens

Pink froth
    covers the bottom
        of the cloud bank
The sun's last brightness
    shimmers from
        beneath the western front
A brief glow
    off the neighbor's
        high windows

Look away
   changed again
     to golden fire
Froth reappears
   white-gold this time
     against the grey
The sun's glorious farewell
   to yet another
     summer day

To be a joy-bearer and a joy-giver
says everything, for in our life, if
one is joyful, it means that one is
faithfully living for God, and that
nothing else counts; and if one
gives joy to others one is doing
God's work; with joy without and
joy within, all is well...I can
conceive no higher way.
~Janet Erskine Stuart
(1857-1914)
English member of Religious
of the Sacred Heart

Part III

JESUS...JOY

What am I doing
    naming a chapter
Jesus...Joy?
The whole earth is full
    of His glory (Isaiah 6:3)
His joy emanates
    from His glory
There is nothing that doesn't
    have the finger print
        of Jesus on it
Actually, Jesus and Joy
    just come together

And it is good!

God's Handiwork

We stand in succession
   from the tiniest molecule
      to the vast cosmos
All varying: size, shape, color, attitude
   of purpose unique
And necessary
   one to another
Knit in a great
   unifying whole

That defies imagination
   or understanding
But rather stands up
   acclaims its Creator
As the great I AM
   the One Who
Calls all things
   into being

As part of this ineffable
   unquenchable stream
Joy swells within my breast
   a great breath of wind
      fills out a sail

The burst of its fullness
brings blessings
Flowing and flooding
and flooding
and flooding
and flooding
the fields

Behold, I say to you, lift up your eyes and look on the fields, that they are white for harvest.

~John 4:35 (NASB)

The Bells
(Written in my trepidation
 before we played)

I wonder, Lord... and
   yet my heart knows
That we re placed
   in Your Place
That our time
   is Your Time
That our joy
   is really, really Your Joy

Thank You, Lord,
   for taking my weakness
And replacing it with
   Your Strength
The "bell gloves" I wear
   are really Your Hands
      over mine
Each bong of each bell
   proclaims Your Glory

BONNNGGG!!!

Music is the thing of the world that I
love most.   ~Samuel Pepys
        (1633-1682)

Great works do not always lie in our
way, but every moment we may do
little ones excellently, this is, with
great love.   ~Francois de Sales
        (1567-1622)

Breakfast Joy-Blessings

I heard Your voice today
   in the early stillness
At first I thought it was one
   of the birdies of the morn
but finally despite my fogginess
   it was as distinct as my own

Calling me to feed
   Your sheep
Now Peter, maybe, but
   not me (John 21:15-17)
But there is Your wonderful watering
   of the Word

I kind of get that but...
   that's not what You mean, is it?
Real food
   that you chew
And swallow and feel stronger
   because of it

What small thing
   can I do?
Hand out breakfast
   boxes to go

A tract rolled in the
    fork-napkin

This tender heart
    just cannot look into
      hopeless eyes
I will dip my eyes
    in love
      coated with joy
And sprinkle joy-blessings
    on breakfast!

Boundless Joy

My lips are trembling
    with Your words
        but I am silent
The bottoms of my feet tingle
    with wanting to dance
        but I am still
My arms reach out
    fingers upward
        praise seeps from my fingertips
I am silently still no more

Your Joy within me
    comes tumbling
Head over heals
    a race of expression
To have tasted unity (John 17:21)
    and remain One
Beyond me
    to comprehend

Joy emanates...radiates
   in the song
     of my soul
Joy dances
   in the Love
     of my heart
Joy embraces
   the children
     for I am ONE
And we are JOY!

In Your presence is fullness of joy
In Your right hand there are
   pleasures forever.

~Psalm 16:11 (NASB)

Cloud-Secret

The clouds race each other
Although Canada's in sight
It's not the finish line

In their enthusiasm to be first
They sprinkle Jesus-Joy along the way
(And you thought it was rain!)

Although the clouds are grey
    on the bottom
Their tops shimmer
    in the sun
Have you seen pictures of angels
    sitting on the clouds?

It's always the cloud tops
    they envision
Well, I'll let you in
    on a cloud-secret
Angels sit quite nicely
    on the grey clouds too

The closer they are
    the better they see

And the quicker to get
　　into the action
I keep my guardian angel
　　very busy

She's extremely good
　　at what she does
Although always on time
　　she often arrives
　　　a bit damp
From Jesus-Joy!

Bayshore Symphony

What delight to hear
   but you'd never guess
      the pleasure in the play
From stoic faces
   ah, I did
      I saw a smile sneak out
I asked my friend
   if she was going to dance
      we could have (10 years ago!)
The instruments were played
   as children's toys
      hats included
Toes tapped
   heads nodded
      all we could do to sit still
What fun!
   ready to listen
to a SERIOUS symphony
Were we in
   for a surprise!
Just a sprinkle
   of Jesus-Joy

In and Out

Joy within
  and Joy without
It makes me want to
  shout about
Him!
And raise my voice
  my hands in praise
To our Glorious God
  Who even puts Joy
    in the tune of the bassoon
And a giggle
  in the toot of the flute
Lay down our too-serious world
  trade a ready-made
    artificial bouquet
For a whole field
  of wild flowers
    to dance in

Enter Jesus

There is an immediacy
    about so many things
But time passes
    and our attention
Focuses on another
    this-needs-to-be-done
RIGHT NOW!

The abiding Love
    of God
Slows us down
    saying
Look here, listen or
    wait for now

I'll show you how
    when time is right
I'll give the words
    if you give the willing
And then...
    and then...

Oh, the Joy of
  obedience
Yes, this but more
The inner abiding
  Joy of Jesus

To rest in His hand
  secure in this
Eternal moment
Without the slippery bookends
  of time

Now, take
  a deep breath
Exhale
  slowly
And once more

Exit troubles,
  pain, sorrow
    stress that peace-stealer
Enter Jesus, there all the time
  kind Friend Restorer of rest
    Eternal Healer
Lay your troubles there
  Where? Right there
    at the foot of the Cross

Humility of Pain

There is something quite lovely
    about the humility of pain
Not the external so much
    but an internal abiding joy
Like a soap bubble bursting
    not splashy but "poof" there
To be part of suffering humanity
    makes room for my pleas

In a variety of ways
    comes this surfacing plea
Things: All I did yesterday
    that I can't do today
      will you...?
Desire for companionship
    I don't want to be alone
      will you...?
Inclusion in suffering
    Can we...? After all we're invited
    to share (I Peter 4:13)

Then there is that internal humility
    that softens the heart
And gives us tenderness
    in new places

Compassion becomes empathy
   caring becomes involvement
God's Love takes on
   human form...again

All this...we have Jesus-eyes
   and Jesus-Joy
How lavish He is
   with His Gifts
I wouldn't trade
   a moment
Of pain

Joy-Sparkle

How easily:
    under the guise of friendship
Even lurking in the glories
    of the sunset
The tempter's
    magnetism takes
Our attention from
    The Holy

Pull of busyness
    desire to please
Time so quickly
    filled and gone
Tarnishes our Lord's
    joy-sparkle
Dampens the reach-out
    for Jesus enthusiasm

Scripture speaks of
    first love lost
When we allow our thoughts
        to wander
            and forget the cost
That Jesus paid
    upon the cross

Oh Lord, return the sparkle
   to Your Joy
For Your glory
   all my creativity employ
Refresh
   renew
Turn my heart
   again to You.

Dear Jesus, don't ever allow me to lose Your Jesus-Joy. The world encroaches and attempts to destroy the wonders of Your Love by gobbling up my time which really is not my own. Remember, Oh Lord, that I am but dust; in my weakness is Your strength; my frail humanity offers evidence to Your majestic glory.

Thank You, Friend Pain

A phrase borrowed from a book
   caused me to pause
      take another look
At my own attitude
   potential ingratitude
Is pain indeed friend or foe?
   remain in faith
      trust what I do not know

The enemy-foe-
   clogs my thoughts
      in a vast undertow
That would pull me down
   and leave me to drown
In a fathomless sea
   of overwhelming self-pity

And in the end
   what is a friend?
One who betters
   for his being
Shares my sorrows
   pulls back the curtain
      that blocks my seeing

So Pain
    I choose to call
    you friend
And thank you
    from this hole
    where I descend
For I really do know
    I will arise
    brokenness made whole

Lord, send me soaring
    from unimaginable depths
    to incomparable heights
That bear the marks
    of humility
And find joy
    not sleeping anymore
    but purring at the door

Thank you
    Friend Pain

Joy Remains

I read poetry
    of autumn colors
Yet I am still filled
    with rainbows of spring
The truth of emptiness
    calls chasm-like
But I am loath to leave
    the wonder, the mystery,
        the fullness...of joy

Joy doesn't leave, Child
    it transforms
Into the fullness
    of empty
When that inmost place
    is void of crass, pride,
        self-stuff, wantonness, fear
When all these take flight
    from the portholes
        of your soul

Joy remains
    sustains
Perhaps hidden
    for a while
In a desert
    sandstorm
To reappear
    sand blasted

Laughing in the
    gleaming of it

The Answer

It seems all my life
    I have quested
Seeking to fill
    this emptiness
You alone
    are my fulfillment
You alone
     ease the sorrow
       of my soul

To my astonishment
    (a word not big enough)
Out of the ashes
    of my life
Arises a thing
    of great beauty
As a swan wings
    its way in first flight

Lament
    transfigures to song
Sadness
    soars joy-saturated

Like a sponge
   that can hold no more
Without overflowing
   spilling, seeping
     gushing until all

Are splashed with
   Jesus-Joy

Beauty For Ashes

...to give unto them beauty for ashes,
the oil of joy for mourning
the garment of praise
for the spirit of heaviness
that they might be called
   trees of righteousness
the planting of the Lord
that He might be glorified
   ~Isaiah 61:3 (KJ)

PHOTOGRAPH CREDITS

Photo on page 73 by Shannon Mihelich, July 2014

Wikipedia Creative Commons
http://commons.wikimedia.org/wiki/Category:Images
Cover page image- 1803-n-hills-knoxsvills-tn1.jpg, Brian Stansbury, 2010.

Part I page 19-Stoneangel, M62, 2007; page 21-German Federal Archive, Refuges, uploaded by B Arch Bot, 2007, page 25-Balloons in the sky.jpg, Chrystal, 2006; page 31-Soap Bubble.jpg, Werner, 2011; page 39-Northern California Yard Sale, 2005; page 40-Music_stub.png, Jain Abhishek, 2012; page 51-Rainbows v.JPG, Szymnguin, 2014; page 54-Kornblume inenem Weizenfeld.jpg, Werner100359.

Part II Sunset in Belo Horizonte, Higor Douglas, 2013; page 65-An Alaskan Sunset, PD US NOAA, uploaded by Saperaud, 2005; page 79-Haliaeetus leucocephalus-Alaska, Ryan McFarland, 2010; page 77-Bohemian Wax Wing, Randen Pederson, 2005; page 83-Eveningshadows, Brookie; page 84-Beach Bean (Canavalia rosea), Bob Peterson from North Palm Beach, Florida, Planet Earth! 2013; page 88-Big Cululononimbus, Frederick M., 2004; page 87-House spar-rows (passer domesticus) eating, Richard001, 2008; page

94-Sunflower with a bee.jpg, François, 2006; page 97-Cynara cardunculus 008 (artichoke), H.Zell, 2011; page 101-Glorius sunset-NOAA.jpg, Commander John Bortniak, (1984) 2005.

Part III Page 105-Wheatfield Strasburg, France, Shizhoa (reviewer), 2012; page 109-Family Interaction, WSU enewsletter, 2011; page 113-Spring-geograph.org.uk-481805.jpg, Bernard Bradley, 2007; page 119-Service dog for boy with autism, Zipster, 2013.

GNU Free Documentation License
http://en.wikipedia.org/wiki/
GNU_Free_Documentation_License
Back cover image-maple tree in Wilsonville, Oregon, M.O. Stevens, Autumn 2007; page 31-Persian Cat sleeping in a basket, Sabius, 2008.

Quotation Credits
Some of the older quotes found in this book are taken from *The Doubleday Christian Quotation Collection*, compiled by Hannah Ward and Jennifer Wild, 1997. Permission is obtained to use lyrics from Big Daddy Weave, *page 67, I am redeemed* and page 62-3, JohnDenver lyrics, *Sunshine on my Shoulders*.

THE AUTHOR:

M ary Mueller lives in the beautiful Pacific Northwest. Retired special education teacher, gardener, mother of two daughters, grandmother of seven, she is most of all a child of God. She claims that if this is all that distinguishes her, it is more than enough.

CPSIA information can be obtained at www.ICGtesting.com
Printed in the USA
BVOW11s0030080115

382223BV00002B/3/P